The Joy of Mah Jong
(or **Mah Jiang Joy**)

By

Tong Seng Tjoa, M.D.

AuthorHouse™
1663 Liberty Drive
Bloomington, IN 47403
www.authorhouse.com
Phone: 1-800-839-8640

First published by AuthorHouse 09/23/2011

ISBN: 978-1-4567-6376-3 (sc)
ISBN: 978-1-4567-6375-6 (ebk)

Library of Congress Control Number: 2011908039

To

my beloved parents,
I owe immeasurable gratitude

Half of the proceeds will be donated to
Chuang Yen Monastery in Kent, New York
where my parents have rested in peace

Contents

Mah Jong Set and Accessories

A complete set would have the following tiles & accessories:

A total of 144 picture tiles: comprising

A. Decorative tiles (8):

a. Flower tiles

          Plum   Orchid Chrysanthemum Bamboo

One of each for a total of four tiles; and

b. Season tiles

           Spring   Summer   Fall   Winter

One of each for a total of four tiles.

Note: Different manufacturers may design different symbols. I called them decorative because these tiles do not participate in the formation of sets in the Hand and are instantly exposed upon their acquisition. Their inclusions are purely for bonus *fans* (points) in the total point count and their acquisition is more luck dependent rather than skill. For example, each decorative tile represents to belong to a player <u>during a play</u>. Thus,

Plum & Spring, designated both as #1of the two series respectively, are recognized as belonging to the current wind <u>Position Leader</u> East, which is a roving position. This follows that

Orchid & Summer both as #2, are for South,
Chrysanthemum & Fall both as #3, are for West and
Bamboo & Winter both as #4, are for North in respective reference to wind position leader East during every play of a Hand.

In contrast, and for comparison, the first designated Leader East <u>seat</u>, elected at the start of a game and known as the Home Base, is permanent during a game.

B.   Suit (numbered) tiles:

a.   Bamboos[1]

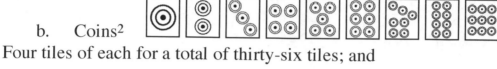

Four tiles of each for a total of thirty-six tiles; and

b.   Coins[2]

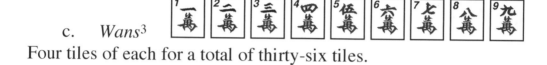

Four tiles of each for a total of thirty-six tiles; and

c.   *Wans*[3]

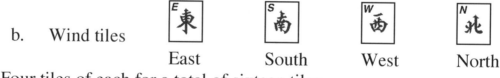

Four tiles of each for a total of thirty-six tiles.

Note: These three suit tiles (36) are collectively known as numbered tiles (*shu pai*).

C.   Word tiles (*zi pai*):

.   a.   Virtue tiles[4]

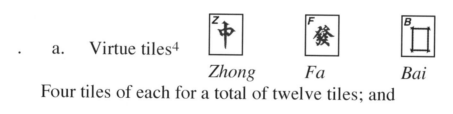

Zhong   Fa   Bai

Four tiles of each for a total of twelve tiles; and

b.   Wind tiles

East   South   West   North

Four tiles of each for a total of sixteen tiles.

Adding all these tiles together will give a grand total of 144 playing tiles. Excluding the decorative tiles, the three numbered (bamboo, coin & *wan*) and two word (virtue & wind) tiles are known as the five basic "component" tiles of the game. A good set will also provide a couple of blank tiles as replacements in case of loss.

---

[1] Known as "bams" to American players. Bamboo 1 is usually a picture of bird.

[2] Described as "dots" or "circles" by other authors

[3] *Wan* means ten thousand for the common word character on the tiles. Known as "cracks" among American players.

[4] *Zhong* means center, *Fa* means expansion and *bai* means white or symbol for purity. Collectively known to American players as Red, Green & white dragon based on their face colors respectively.

I.   Position Wind Leader East indicator

The dice, which is always in the possession of the contemporaneous East Leader for casting to start a play, has replaced a separate device to symbolize this position. This roving East Leader is independent of the wind of the round (round wind), which is the same for all players during the course of a round. The changing of the round wind occurs when the *first* elected Position Leader East player regains the dice at the end of a round of plays.

II.   Home Base indicator

This device is not a necessity. However, if available, it is given to the *first* elected Position Wind Leader East, whose seat selection is a one-time process at the start of a game. for safe keeping during the game. It is just a reminder as to where the game started and where the changing of the round of the wind takes place.

III.   Wind indicator

This device comes in different designs and shapes by different manufacturers of sets. It is used to indicate the current round of the wind (round wind) at any given play of a round. Each facet will indicate only one wind at a time: East, South, West & North in this order. The duty of changing of wind round is bestowed on the occupant of the Home Base for safe keeping as well as that of an announcer for the wind change when this *First* elected Position Leader East regains possession of the dice at the completion of a round.

IV.   Chips of different sizes and colors are used to represent different monetary values, for example, 1, 5, 10 and 100 unit denominators with an equal base capital for all players for payment at time of settlements during a game.

V.   Dice

These are the familiar six-face cubes devices used in many diverse games of chance. They are numbered individually on each side 1 through 6. The possession of which is always with the contemporaneous Position Leader East–the player who casts the dice to start a play. A complete set usually provides at least a pair of dice.

VI.   Rulers of approximate equal length of the side of a wall (18 tile long), will come in handy for those with unsteady hands. They can be used for straightening and pushing forwards the built walls and make counting unnecessary. A regular ruler will serve nicely for this purpose. A good

9

set will have all these accessories in a sturdy container that is easy and light to carry.

Terminology

To make my instruction for learning the game easier to follow, the reader is encouraged to first familiarize him/her-self with the following nomenclature which is my distinctive creation and has exclusively been used in my earlier books: **Mah Jpng for Everyone** for the novice, **Mah Jong Unlimited** and **Mah Jong Fun**. Chinese terms are given in *italic*.

Active Wall   This is the wall to the left of the break site, and where the tiles are drawn at the start, and during the course of a play.

Inactive Wall   This is the wall to the right of the break site. The tiles from this wall serve as replacements for the decorative (flower/season) tiles and after exposing a set of *gang*.

Leader   Is meant the Position Wind Leader East – the player with the dice at the start of every play, disputably called "Dealer" by all other authors. Since tiles of a mahjong Hand are not dealt by this player but drawn by each individual player following this player-leader's turn.

Home Base (Permanent Leadership Seat)   Is the designated seat of the *first* elected position wind leader East. The occupant of this seat is concurrently the first to start the game. This is the site where the change of the wind round takes place. It is permanent for the duration of a game. The Wind Indicator device, is permanently placed with this *first* elected Position Leader East, can also be used to serve at the same time as Home Base indicator.

Position Leader East   Is the player who assumes the duty to throw the dice to start the play as Position Wind Leader East. Each player's *wind* position is relative to this Leader East's Position. And every player will assume this position at least once in every round. The following diagram shows the difference of wind position between

Mah Jong   and   <u>Compass:</u>

	West			**<u>North</u>**	
North		South	West		East
	<u>East</u>			South	

Note: The East, South, West and North position for Mah Jong (counter-clockwise) does not follow the direction of the compass (clockwise) except for the maintenance of the position of the opposing wind position. Customarily, we use East as the orientation position in a game. In contrast, North is the customarily referenced point for compass, as it is in the game of contract bridge.

Game Made up of 4 rounds of wind change.

Round Consists of at least 4 plays, assuming none of the players repeats his/her position as Position (Wind) Leader East.

Hand Is defined as each player's total number of tiles for feature building, based on his/her own blueprint. It consists of 13 during a play and 14 tiles upon *mahjong* in the classic version. Extra tiles from decorative (flower/season) and 4th tile from *gang* are excluded from the total count of fourteen.

Set Is defined as either a group of sequence, *peng, gang* or pair.

Peng Is a set of three identical tiles. This is the Mandarin pronunciation for *pong* or *pung* that are dialects of different parts of China and used by various authors.

Gang Is formed with four identical tiles. I adopt, for the same reason, the official (Mandarin) pronunciation for this set that replaced *kong* or *kang* used in other mahjong books.

Coin My preferred description for one of the suits rather than "dot" or "circle" as described by other authors.

Wan Is the true meaning of the Chinese word for "ten thousand" engraved on the tile. Popularly known among the American players as "crack".

Virtue The word I use to denote collectively the three Chinese character *zhong* (center), *fa* (prosperity). and *bai* (white=purity). These tiles, together with all wind tiles are grouped as belonging to the word tiles. The colors on the tile characters are usually red, green and white (blank) respectively.

Dragon Three sets of sequential numerical order of suit (bamboo, coin & *wan*) tiles from 1 through 9, either in same or 3 different suits. This is the true meaning of the Chinese word and the original term for one of the adopted entities (features).

End (External =Terminal) tiles   The 1s & 9s of the three suit tiles.

Hard Tiles   Are meant for the word (virtue and wind) tiles. For practical and statistical point of view, all end tiles (1s & 9s) are considered belonging to this group.

Soft (Internal = Middle) Tiles   Are tiles made up of the 2s through 8s of the three (numbered) suits.

Raw tiles   Are tiles not found on the playing field, either as discarded or exposed in claimed sets

Dead tiles   Tiles that have been discarded or claimed by a player in forming sets of sequence, *peng* or *gang,* and hence no longer available.

Hidden (Concealed) tiles   Are tiles that are hidden from other players' view, in other words, those in each player's Hand.

Exposed tiles   Tiles that are visible in the playing field either as discards or among the claimed sets.

Replacement tile   Is a tile that a player needs to draw from the inactive wall to replace a decorative (flower/season) or after exposing a set of *gang* before discarding.

Last five tiles   Are the total number of tiles remaining in the wall, which has now been reduced to a single wall. This is only of importance as a warning to all players for sole responsibility of payments to the winner if a player discards a *raw* tile that leads to a player's *mahjong.*

Last tile   Is the tile meant when *all* but one tile of the remnant wall have been drawn, in contrast to some version, where 14 tiles will be left untouched.

Losing tile   A discarded tile that instantly leads to a player's *mahjong,* It is known as a **Winning tile** in the event of **Self-pick**.

Short handed   Denotes a player's Hand with less than thirteen tiles total in the play. Despite the fact that this player can no longer *mahjong*, he/she continues to participate in the play and is bound by the same game rules and responsibilities.

Excess   Indicates a Hand of having more than thirteen tiles, except for the Leader East who has fourteen before making the first discard to start the play. Same game rules apply.

Claim   Is the privilege for any one player to claim a discarded tile at that moment, that is,

    a.   when he/she is to *mahjong*, (*hu*) or

    b.   to form a set of *peng* or *gang* in combination with the two or three tiles in his/her Hand respectively, or

    c.   to complete a sequence. However, making a sequence, in contrast to other claims, can only be claimed by the player whose turn it is to draw next.

Pao   Is the Chinese colloquial term for warning. A player announces *pao* to alert the players, out of courtesy, when he/she exposes at that moment the third set of **One Suit**, or the second set of ***Peng (Gang)* a Virtue**, irrespective of the true composition of the concealed tiles in Hand. This means when a discard of the "pre-warned" tile leads to this alerting player's immediate completion, the perpetrator is held *sole* responsible in payments for all players. But if the Hand turns out not to be of **one suit**, nor <u>three</u> sets of ***Peng* a Virtues**, (i.e. two *pengs* & a pair), the "discarder" of the "claimed" tile is absolved of sole responsibility in payments to the winner. However, in the event that the announcer of *pao* claims the tile only to form an exposed set, the risk-taking player will be responsible for payments later to the winner for **Self-pick** of the winning tile.

Feature   Denotes a certain set of pair, group, combination, or "act". Each set is given a specific Intrinsic *Fan* Value (IFV) to play for and can be found on an agreed, codified list, comparable to the options of extra features in a basic model car.

Entity   Is an adopted feature to play for with an assigned <u>intrinsic value</u> of one or more *fans*. All the adopted entities are codified on an IFV List and which all players have approved prior to the start of a game.

Fan   The assigned intrinsic unit value of an adopted entity expressed in Mandarin Chinese. It is called ***tai*** in Taiwanese. It is universally known as a unit point.

Mahjong ***Hu***, so pronounced in Manderin Chinese. I use it here as a verb to mean the completion of the requirement of one of the fundamentals for a play, colloquially expressed as going out, or complete.

The Goal of a *mahjonged* Hand

To achieve one of the following three fundamental features:

I.   Basic Configuration

To establish 4 sets of well-defined groups of either sequence(s), *peng(s)* or *gang(s)* and *a pair*, a basic pattern of 4 x 3 (4) + 2. For example,

sequences   set of three same

suit tiles in numerical order

peng   set of three identical tiles

gang   set of four identical tiles

pair   set of two identical tiles

Comment: All quoted sets above in this *mahjonged* Hand are either completed from a discard or self-picked during the course of a play, with the understanding that whenever the third member of a set, which is acquired from a discard (or the fourth for a set of three in Hand to form *gang*), the resulting set is instantly exposed. The pair set is always self-picked unless the second member of the pair is the calling tile to *mahjong*.

Note: A set of *gang* is not required as a component feature to *mahjong*. When a player obtains the fourth tile of an earlier acquired, exposed set of *peng*, he/she has the option to keep it in Hand for use in other set combination or add to convert the earlier exposed set of *peng* into *gang*. In this instance, the player will concurrently draw a replacement tile from the inactive wall before making a discard. No player can keep four identical tiles hidden in Hand as set of *gang*, unless the player splits it into two pairs as components of **Seven Pairs**, or use them separately in sets to form the entity **Quads**. (see terminology)

To reiterate, the requirement for a player to *mahjong* is to compose a Hand of this basic pattern of either all sets of sequences, or all *pengs,* or all *gangs* <u>plus</u> a pair of this first fundamental. The winning tile is the one tile that completes the composition of above example set combination.

II.   **Seven Pairs**

To collect seven pairs of any combination of suit, virtue or wind tiles. For example: a completed Hand is composed of the following tiles:

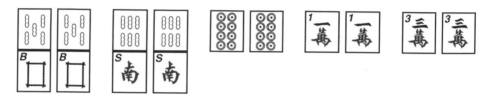

Comment: The winning (waiting) tile is the second mate of a pair that completes the final pair among these tiles. It should be understood that all the pairs forming the composition of this Hand are hidden in Hand.

III.   **Thirteen Masters**

To assemble one of each of 1 & 9 of the three suits (bamboo, coin & *wan*), one of each of the virtue (*zhong, fa & bai*) and one of each of the wind (east, south, west & north) tiles. To the enthusiasts of the game, this is the crowning of a most exciting as well as enviable entity. To wit,

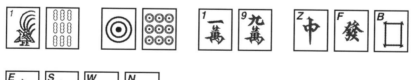

and one of these tiles to form the pre-requisite pair.

Note: This waiting (ready) Hand offers the most number of chances to *mahjong,* namely, 3 x 13 minus all visible dead tiles on the playing field, not counting the unknown number of concealed tiles in Hand of other players.

For those readers who are interested in learning additional variants and fundamentals, I have the pleasure to refer them to my books **Mah Jong Fun** (2003), **Mah Jong For Everyone** (**Novice**) and pending second edition of **Mah Jong Unlimited** (2000).

Entities

The following features are my suggested basic Entities, each is given an assigned intrinsic *fan* (point) value (IFV). They are the components and contributors of *fans* to be <u>added</u> together in the computation of a Hand's value upon *mahjong*. It is comparable to the separate value of the added options for a basic priced car. I made an exception for two special Hands, namely, **Earthly Charm** and **Heavenly Grace**. Their total value is similar to one packaged price to include all the options for a top of-the-line car.

Most of the following entities have also been mentioned in my earlier published books, **Mah Jong Unlimited** and my latest **Mah Jong Fun.**

ONE *FAN* (POINT)

1. **Position (Own) Flower Tile**
   The flower/season tile corresponds to the player's *wind* position.

2. *Peng* **Position (Own) Wind Tile**
   The set corresponds to a player's *wind* position in relation to the current Leader <u>East</u>'s Position.

3. *Peng* **Prevalent Wind**.
   The formed set is the *wind of the round* independent of a player's wind position.

4. *Peng* **a Virtue**
   Any one set of the following:

5. **Eye Pair 2**, **5**, or **8**. Any one
   Pair of **2-2**,   **5-5**,   or   **8-8** of any suit tiles

6. **Chopped (No Ends)**
   Hand contains only the so-called soft or middle (2s – 8s) tiles, thus excludes 1's & 9's and no virtue or wind tiles in any set, upon *mahjong*:

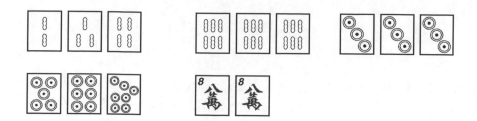

Note: This completed Hand reveals in addition the **Eye Pair** (*wan* 8) entity.

7.   **All Sequences**

Hand completed on melded sets of any combination of the three suits, thus no sets of *peng* or *gang* from wind and/or virtue tiles.

8.   **Exposed** or **Hidden** *Gang* *

The difference between these two is that the fourth member of *gang* is claimed from a discard. With a hidden version, the player self-picked all four tiles for the set. In certain versions by prior agreement, its identity may remain a secret when exposing them, and may be codified as an entity with a separate IFV of two (x) *fans*.

9.   **Twin Pairs** (**Two Identical Pairs**)

Two identical pairs of suit (numbered) or word tiles, either virtue or wind tiles.

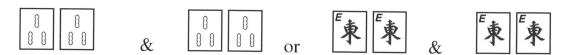

10.   **Twin Sisters** (**Double Sequences**)

Two sets of identical numerical order of any suit tiles:

11.   **Twin Brothers** (**Double Brother** *Peng* **Sets**)

Two sets of *peng* of the <u>same denominators</u> of suit tiles.

Note: I use <u>sister</u> for set of <u>sequence</u>, and <u>brother</u> for *peng* with equal IFV.

12. Quad in Two

The following example shows four bamboo 3 or any numbered suit tiles used in two sets:

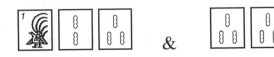

13. Young & Old

It is composed of sets of sequence of 1-2-3 and 7-8-9 of the *same* suit.

14. Juniors & Seniors

It is a combination of sets of *peng* of 1-1-1 and 9-9-9 of any same suit tiles

15. Ying Yang (Two Suits)

The completed Hand is a composition of any two of the three numbered suits.

16. Clean (Front Door)

The player has no exposed sets upon *mahjong*. Exposed *gang* and decorative (flower/season) tiles do not violate the spirit of this entity, because their exposure is mandatory.

17. Self-pick

The player picks the winning tile him/herself.

18. Single

The winning **x** tile as a feature for single is valid in the following examples:

    a.   1-2-**x** (3) or (7)-**x**- 8-9

    b.   3-**x** (4)-5

    c.   for the missing pre-requisite pair: s-**x** (s), v-**x** (v) or w-**x** (w) where
            s = suit, v = virtue or w = wind tile,

d. 3-4-5-6, where **x** can be either a 3 or 6 as the group can be viewed as sets of 3-**x** (3) & 4-5-6 or 3-4-5 & 6-**x** (6),

e. 6-8-8-8, the calling tile **x** can be either a 6 or 7 based on the set formation of 6-**x** & 8-8-8 or better still, 6-**x**-8 & 8-8, but for

f. 7-8-9-9. This group of tiles can be viewed as having sets of the configurations of either 7-8-9 & 9-**x** (9), or (6) **x**-7-8-**x** (9) & 9-9. Thus, the only single calling tile applicable for this entity is 9, because in the second instance, two calling tiles do not fulfill the criteria of calling single as defined in the above examples.

19. Orphan

The winning tile is the *last* available tile to *mahjong*. The winning fourth tile for the twin pair in the formation of **Seven Pairs** in Hand and the robbery of *gang* tile are legit for this entity. **Self-pick** is a valid additional contributor of *fans*.

20. Par

The winning tile is the 4th discarded tile by the north player on the playing field. This player may claim this same entity plus any codified entity(ies), if he/she *mahjongs* on the drawn tile. This is the 4th occasion for any player to go out

21. Piracy (*Gang* Robber)

The winning tile is claimed from the possessor who is caught in the "act" of adding the relevant tile to his/her exposed *peng*. In this instance, **Orphan** will be an added feature and additional *fan* for Hand's total value.

22. Poverty

Completed Hand is devoid of decorative, set of *peng* of virtue and/or prevalent/position wind tiles. This entity is excluded from the IFV list if the decorative tiles are not included in the game.

TWO *FANS*

1. Monocle

Mahjonged on the second mate of the **Eye Pair**. For example,
    2-**x**,   **5**-**x**   or   **8**-**x** of any suit tile.

2. **Mixed Ends**

    All sets and the pair must include 1's, 9's, virtue and/or wind tiles known as the hard (terminal) tiles upon *mahjong*. The sets may be a mixture of sequence or *peng/gang*.

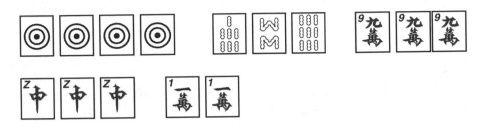

Note: The IFV of each set of **Peng** Virtue tiles above is to be added to the total *fan* count of the winning Hand. If the sequence set of 7-8-9 bamboo is a set of *peng* of 9 bamboo, then **Threesomes** entity can also be claimed.

3. **Mixed Dragon**

    The three sequence sets forming the **Dragon** entity must be made up of three different suits:

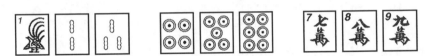

4. **Mixed Triple Sisters (Sequences)**

    Similar sets so formed must be of three different suit combination:

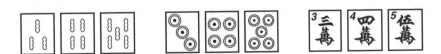

5. **Quad in Three (Sets)**

    Four tiles of one denominator of the same suit: bamboo, or coin, or *wan*, used in three ways, The following example shows the common denominator of bamboo 5,

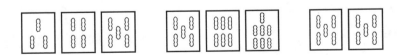

6. **Blessing**

    The winning tile is a replacement tile after drawing a decorative tile or set of *gang*. In the event that this tile is another decorative tile or the 4th tile of a second *gang*, a suitable substitute term would be **Gang** on **Gang**. This could imply that the

IFV of this entity is additive for the consecutive draw until picking the winning tile, for example, *2fs* (first draw) + 1x + 1x etc. rare occurrence, but it did happen.

Note: Compare **Blossom Picker** (*mahjong* on specific coin tile). For mnemonic purpose, both entities start with the letter B.

7. **Birdie**

The winning tile is the 3rd discarded tile by the West player on the playing field when a player *mahjongs*. For the same reason, this entity is also applicable for the west player self on completing the winning Hand at his/her first turn to draw (the 3rd occasion) The player is reminded to include all the IFV of codified entities for the total *fan* count including **Virgin** entity.

8. **Miracle**

The winning tile is drawn from the <u>last</u> tile of the remaining wall.

Note: In contrast to some other versions, my last tile means when all tiles of the walls have been exhausted and not the tile next to the last 14 tiles which will not be

used.   Compare **Moon Snatcher** (*mahjong* on specific coin tile. To ease memory, both start with the letter M.

9. **Solo**

Winning on the second mate of a <u>remaining</u> tile in a <u>waiting</u> Hand. This implies that four sets (twelve tiles) of the Hand have been exposed.

10. **Home Run**

A player *mahjongs* on the last discard by the last player of the play.

11. ***Gang on Gang***

This entity is recognized when the winning tile is the result of a second replacement tile. It's IFV is additive to the number of replacements after more than once. This means that after 2nd replacements, its IFV increases to 3.

12. **Basic *Mahjong***

Is meant when a completed Hand is devoid of codified entities such as the possession of ***Peng* Prevalent** or **Position (Own)** Wind tiles, and set formation of

Single, **Eye Pair**, **Chopped** and other combinations. However, entities resulted from special circumstances such as **Self-pick**, **Virgin**, **Ace**, **Eagle**, **Gem**, are legit examples for additional *fans* towards total *fan* count.

Note: The inclusion of this entity to the List depends on whether there is no minimum *fan* count for a a *mahjonged* Hand and so does its IFV may be subjected to negotiation prior to the start of a game.

THREE *FANS*

1.   **Lucky Strike**
     The player **Self-picks** the winning tile with a **Clean Front Door** Hand (no exposed set of sequence or *peng*).

Note: Since the exposure of flower/season or set of *gang* tiles is mandatory, this entity is still valid under this circumstance. It is also applicable when the set of exposed *peng* has been converted into *gang*. The Hand is, as it were, closed. All codified entities in the winning Hand are to be included and same computation of *fan* count applies.

2.   **Eagle**
     A player *mahjongs* on the <u>2nd</u> discarded tile of the play by the south player. Compare entity **Gem**, which is the given name when the south player <u>self-picks</u> the winning tile.

3.   **(Pure) Dragon**
     3 Sets of sequential number of any same suit tiles:

4.   **(Pure) Triple Sisters (Sequences)**
     Three identical sets of <u>one</u> suit.

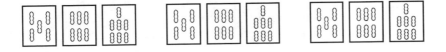

5.   **Triplet (Triple Brothers)**
     Three sets of *pengs* of the <u>same denominator</u>.

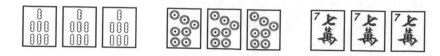

6. Pure Ends

All sets must contain sets of 1's or 9's of suit tiles, either as sequences or *peng/gang* and including the pre-requisite pair, thus no word tiles.

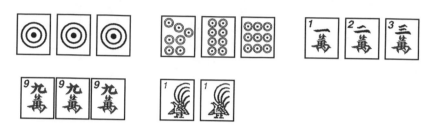

7. Dwarfs (All Small)

No tile in formed sets has numerical order higher than 4:

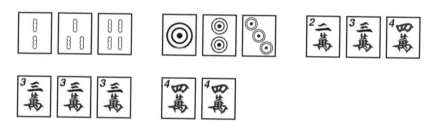

Note: This completed Hand reveals **Quad in Two** (*wan* 3) entity. Had coin 1 been timely replaced with coin 4 prior to *mahjong*, either from a claim of discard or self pick before its exposure, total *fan* count could be increased with the addition of IFV from **Three Numbers** (2s, 3s & 4s), **Triple Sisters** (2-3-4 b c w), and **Chopped** (no end tiles). Further increase would still be possible if *peng wan* 3 could be converted into sequence of 2-3-4. The Hand would then have added entities of **Relatives by 4**, **Identical Twin** (2-3-4 *wan*), **Quad in Three** (*wan* 4) and **Sequences**!

8. Giants (All Big)

All tiles in sets belong to numbered suit 6 and higher:

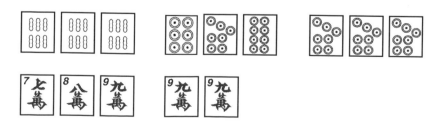

Note: This completed Hand reveals also **Quad in Two** for coin 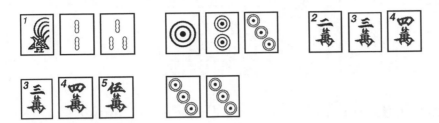 tile.

9.   **Relatives by X**

All sets share a common denominator (**X**) and is determined by the pre-requisite pair. The common denominator for the following group sets are suit tiles:

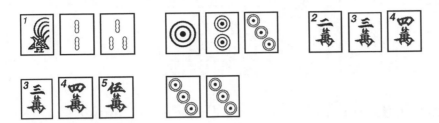

Note: Replacing *wan* 4 and 5 in the sets 2-3-4 & 3-4-5 with 1 and 2 respectively, will create additional entities such as **Dwarfs** (4 and below) and **Pure Triple Sisters** (1-2-3 b c *w*). An experienced player would have aimed ahead all these potential features during the course of a play and would have sensed the exhilarating excitement when a player could achieve this undertaking!

10.   **Quad in Four**

In the following example, bamboo 6 (or any other numbered tile) is shown used in <u>four</u> different sets:

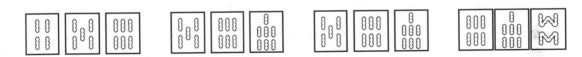

Note: IFV of such entity (**Quad**) is always one *fan* less than the formed sets.

11.   **Double Twin Sisters (Sequences)**

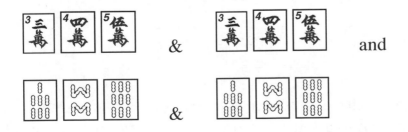

Comment: Applicable for any 2 suit combination. When none of the sets has been exposed my reader is well advised to aim for **Seven Pairs** entity which has greater IFV with a required additional pair for completion.

12.   Double Twin Brothers

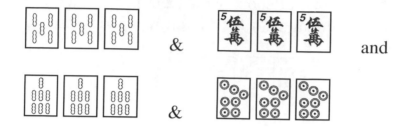

Comment: Playing for this entity, potential additional entities besides the formed **Threesomes**, could come from among other **Chopped**, **Two** or **Three Numbers**, to name the apparent few, depending on the required set of pair.

13.   Double Young & Old

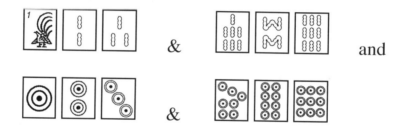

Note: Applicable to any <u>two suit</u> combination.

14.   Double Juniors & Seniors

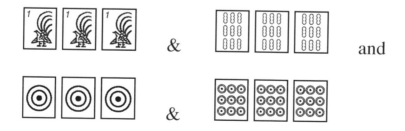

Note: Not limited to these two suit combination for this entity. The winning player of such a Hand should thus not forget to include the IFV of all applicable entities on the agreed list.

Note: Please keep in mind that I don't always describe the full composition of the Hand when I give examples of codified entities.

FIVE *FANS*

1. **Bouquet**
   Denotes <u>one</u> complete series of Flower or season tiles:

Flower   Plum   Orchid Chrysanthemum   Bamboo   <u>or</u>

Season   Spring   Summer   Fall   Winter

2. **Gem**
   The south player **Self-picks** the winning tile on his/her very <u>first</u> turn to draw a tile after the leader East's first discard to start a play. Compare with an **Eagle** entity.

Note: The IFV of **Virgin** and all adopted entities in Hand are valid for the total *fan* count.

3. **Threesomes** (All *Pengs*)
   Four sets of *pengs/gangs* of any group of tiles and a pair to *mahjong*:

   X-X-X (X), & Y-Y-Y(Y), & Z-Z-Z (Z), & V-V-V (V) and W-W

Note: Compare this with **Hidden Treasure** (All sets of *pengs* are self-picked).

4. ***Peng* Minor Virtues**
   Combined group of two sets of *pengs* and a pair:

5. **Harmonious Mix**

A completed Hand composed of sets of a suit in combination with either Virtue and/or Wind tiles, so called the word tiles:

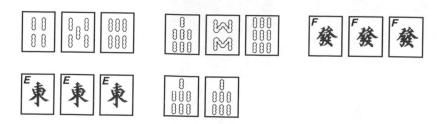

Note: The set of **Peng a Virtue** and applicable **Wind** entity has its own IFV.

6.   Rainbow

The five groups bamboo, coin, *wan*, virtue and wind of tiles must each be represented in a set in any form:

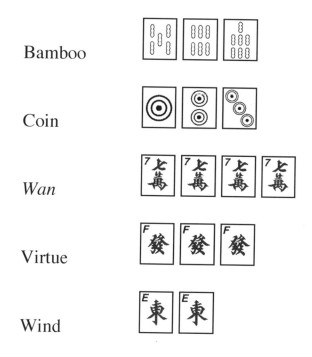

Bamboo

Coin

Wan

Virtue

Wind

Note: Additional *fan(s)* for applicable entities are from **Peng a Virtue** or **Peng Prevalent/Position (Own) Wind** tiles. Other potential entities such as calling **Single**, **Orphan**, among others, in the list of agreed entities, should not be forgotten in calculating the total *fan* count!

7.   Family of Fives

The four formed sets and the pre-requisite pair contain the **common denominator** 5 tiles:

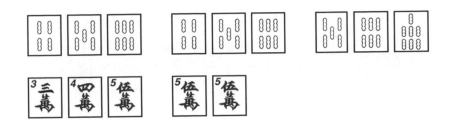

Quiz: What is the value of this Hand? The final score should include in addition, the sum of all other IFV of entities such as **Sequences, Twin, Chopped, Yin Yang,** and **Eye Pair 5**. Timely replacement of bamboo 7 with a 4 and *wan* 3 with a 6, the entities of **three numbers, Pure (Identical) Triple Sisters (Sequences)**, would also be created. Depending on the calling tile and the final completion of the play, **Monocle, Orphan, Solo, Single, Miracl**e and **Self-pick** are all potential entities!

8. **Three Numbers**
   Sets limited to 3 common denominators. For example,

E1.

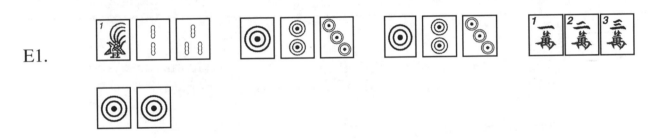

Note: The **Three Numbers: 1, 2 & 3** suit tiles. The IFV of every adopted entities in the Hand are also to be included in the total *fan* count. These are, **Dwarfs, Relatives by 1, Mixed Triple Sisters (Sequences)** (123 b c & w), **Pure Ends, Quad in Three** (4 x c 1), **Twin** (123 c x 2), **Sequences**. Other possible entities and not limited to, are **Single, Self-pick,** and **Orphan**.

E2

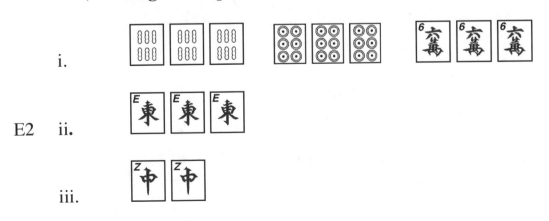

i.

ii.

iii.

Note: The **Three Numbers**: suit, virtue & wind tiles. The IFV of **Threesomes, Triplet,** *Peng* **a Virtue** and applicable **Wind** entities are separately to be included.

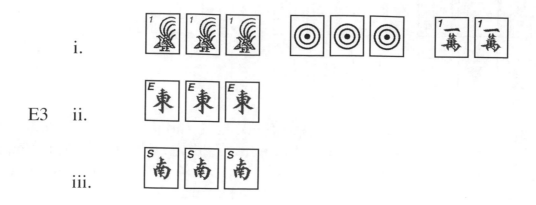

i.

E3 ii.

iii.

Note: The **Three Numbers**: suit of 1s, east & south wind tiles. Similarly, the entities **Threesomes, Mixed Ends** and applicable *Peng* **Prevalent** and/or **Position Wind** entity are all contributors of *fans*.

9.   **Blossom Picker**[5]

The player draws the <u>specific</u> coin ⬚ tile from the inactive wall as a replacement tile to *mahjong*. See also **Blessing** for comparison.

10.   **Moon Snatcher**[6]

This entity is reserved for the player who draws the <u>specific</u> coin ⬚ tile from the <u>last</u> tile of the walls to *mahjong*. Compare **Miracle**, to ease memory, both entities begin with letter M.

SEVEN *FANS*

1.   **Splendid Seven (Seven Pairs)**
Seven pairs of any combination of tiles.

Note: It is self-evident that **Single** or **Clean (Front Door)** entities cannot be claimed, except **Lucky Strike (Self-pick)** However, claim for any of other adopted

---

[5] The origin of this Chinese expression is derived from the imaginary semblance of coin 5 with that of plum flower petals.

[6] "To scoop the moon up from the bottom of the sea" is the expression given by comparing coin 1 as the moon and the playing field within the walls as the sea.

entities such as **Eye Pair**, **Ying Yang**, **Chopped**, **Orphan**, among others, are allowed.

2. Hidden Treasures

The Hand has four sets of hidden _pengs_ (or exposed _gang_), to claim this entity. The entity will otherwise be changed to that of **Threesomes**. To be valid, only the second mate of the calling pre-requisite pair may be claimed from a discard to _mahjong_. In this last instance, the Hand has 4 sets of <u>self-picked</u> _pengs_ and goes out on single north wind tile.

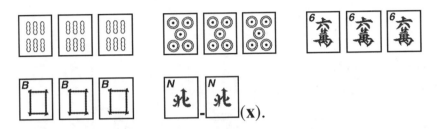

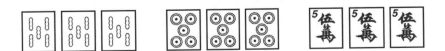

Note: However, when the winning tile in the above example is from a discard to complete the third member of a set of _peng_ to _mahjong_, the applicable entity becomes that of **Threesomes**, because not all sets of _pengs_ in Hand are derived from self-pick. Beside the added _fan_ from entity **Peng a Virtue**, this completed Hand also reveals a **Rainbow** entity.

EIGHT _FANS_

1. *Peng* Major Virtues

Note: The IFV of other adopted entities are to be added in the completed
Hand.

2. Two Numbers

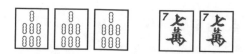

Note: Only suit tiles can form this entity and in **Threesomes**. Certain authors consider virtue and wind tiles as one number in their respective group, which of course, makes no sense. Don't forget to include the IFV of **Triplet** and **Chopped** inthe total *fan* count upon *mahjong*.

TEN *FANS*

1. **Garden of Flowers**
   Denotes two complete series of both Flower & Season tiles:

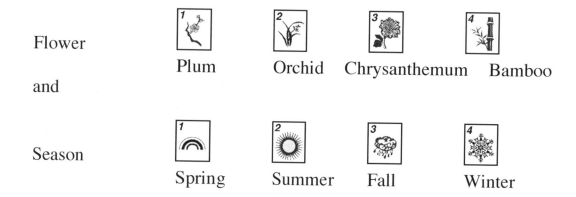

Flower

Plum   Orchid   Chrysanthemum   Bamboo

and

Season

Spring   Summer   Fall   Winter

Note: Upon acquisition of the 8th flower in accomplishing this entity, the player may claim immediate *mahjong* irrespective of his/her readiness of the Hand, and receives from each player double payment because it is always **self-pick**. I do not endorse the version of other authors that the possessor of seven flower/season tiles is entitled to claim the eighth from any player who has the misfortune in its acquisition and is obligated to expose the doomed tile. (I fear it will only encourage dishonesty by keeping it hidden in Hand)

2. **Pure Breed (One Suit)**
   A.   **Royal Jade** (All Bamboos)
   B.   **Perfect Coins** (All Coins)
   C.   **Imperial Red** (All *Wans*) For example,

3. **Virtuous Winds**

Formed sets are composed of virtue and wind tiles in any combination. Each IFV of every respective entity is counted separately for the total *fan* count, this include *Peng* minor **Virtues** in the following example and applicable wind entity:

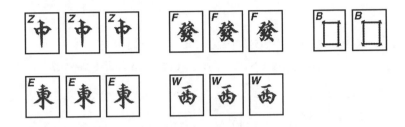

4. **Virgin**

This entity is for the player who declares his/her readiness from the outset of a play by placing his/her tiles face down. This player thus waives his/her right to exchange any drawn tile from the active wall with tiles in his/her Hand or claim any discard <u>except</u> to expose a *gang* or decorative flower/season tile, and to *mahjong*. The player is allowed to change his/her decision in the course of play by disclaiming this entity.

5. **Ace**

This entity is reserved for the leader who *mahjongs* immediately with his/her originally drawn (14) tiles. The leader has 14 tiles at the start of a play. Remember?

Note: The IFV of **Virgin** and every adopted entity are to be added to the total *fan* count. Thus, **Basic *Mahjong*** entity is also applicable for featureless Hand.

6. **Hole in One**

This entity may be claimed by any of the other three players on position leader East's first discard to *mahjong*.

FIFTEEN *FANS*

1. **Breeze**

A Hand composed of **three** sets of *pengs/gangs* and a pair of wind tiles. Additional *fan(s)* can be claimed from relevant wind entities. A set of three tiles is needed to *mahjong*.

TWENTY *FANS*

1. **Supreme Splendid Seven (Supreme Seven Pairs)**
   The formed pair sets are limited to all 3 virtue and 4 wind tiles:

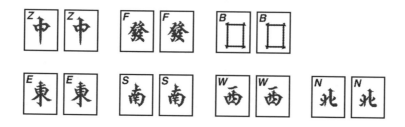

2. **Hurricane**

Note: All wind tile sets must all be in the form of *pengs* or *gang*. An additional pair is needed for completion. Added entities such as **Harmonious Mix**, **Mixed Ends, Threesomes**, **Single** or **Solo** are among the many other potential entities, but not from separate wind entities.

THIRTY *FANS*

1. **Thirteen Masters**

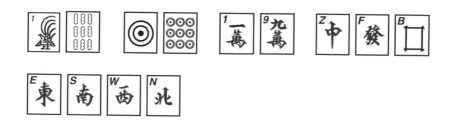

Note: A pre-requisite pair is required to *mahjong* for this Hand. Any of these thirteen tiles may form the pair set for completion. I will draw my reader's attention again that this waiting Hand with this composition would have the greatest number of chances to go out.

FORTY *FANS*

1. **Earthly Charm**
    This fancy Hand composed of **Breeze** and a set of *Peng* End Suit tiles:

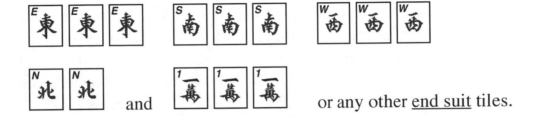

and   or any other <u>end suit</u> tiles.

Note: For the sake of convenience in computing the final *fan* count, I made this special feature a "packaged" entity. Thus the IFV for each adopted basic entity found in the above example (**Threesomes**, **Harmonious Mix**, *Peng* **Position/Prevalent Wind** and **Mixed Ends**) are not to be included again in the computation of the final score. However, in case the set of *peng wan* tiles is composed of sequence, nor of end tiles, then the IFV of each applicable separate entity, such as **Breeze** and **Harmonious Mix** for the computation of the total *fan* count applies.

FIFTY *FANS*

1. **Heavenly Grace**
    This ultimate Hand must be made up of **Hurricane** and a <u>pair</u> of **Virtue**
tiles:

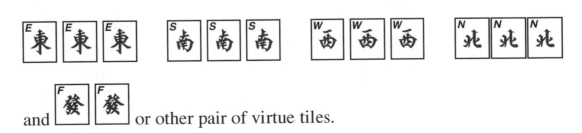

and   or other pair of virtue tiles.

Note: Potential additional *fans* to be included in the computation of the final score are from special entities such as **Self-pick** and **Single (Solo)**. If the pair are not of virtue tiles, or the wind tiles not of four sets of *Pengs,* this entity loses its identity, because this is one of my two *sine quo none* entities. The total *fan* count becomes the sum of all IFV of each adopted entities such as **Breeze** and **Harmonious Mix**.

Comment: Since my own List of Entities with their suggested individual IFV, differs from many other authors, I suggest firstly that an agreeable List be adopted among the players before the start of a game. This is often needed when players are newly acquainted friends.

I hope that my readers have now learned the concept of aiming the best composition, - the creation of most valuable entities, for the Hand to *mahjong*. Of course, a player's success much depends on a player's skill, which is the product of knowledge and experience. This in turn is achieved from practice, and more practice.

Intrinsic *Fan* Value of Tj's List of entities

One *Fan*

1. **Position (Own) Flower**
2. ***Peng* Position (Own) Wind**
3. ***Peng* Prevalent Wind**
4. ***Peng* a Virtue**
5. **Eye Pair**
6. **Chopped**
7. **All Sequences**
8. **Exposed** or **Hidden *Gang***
9. **Twin Pairs**
10. **Twin Sisters**
11. **Twin Brothers**
12. **Quad in Two**
13. **Young & Old**
14. **Juniors & Seniors**
15. **Ying Yang**
16. **Clean Front Door**
17. **Self-pick**
18. **Single**
19. **Orphan**
20. **Par**
21. **Piracy** Compare with entity for ***Gang* on *Gang***[7]
22. **Poverty**

Two*Fans*

1. **Monocle**
2. **Mixed Ends**
3. **Mixed Dragon**
4. **Mixed Triple Sisters**
5. **Quad in Three**
6. **Blessing**[8] Compare ***Gang* on *Gang***

---

7   The winning tile is a consecutive replacement tile from the inactive wall. It also implies its IFV is additive, that is equal to the number of replacement tiles upon *mahjong*.

8   The winning tile is drawn as a replacement tile for decorative tile or *gang* from the inactive wall. IFV for **Self-pick** has been included.

7. **Birdie**
8. **Miracle**
9. **Solo**
10. **Home Run**
11. *Gang* on *Gang*
12. **Basic Mahjong**

Three *Fans*

1. **Lucky Strike**
2. **Eagle**
3. **Pure Dragon**
4. **Mixed Triple Sisters**
5. **Triplet (Triple Brothers)**
6. **Pure Ends**
7. **Dwarfs (All Small)**
8. **Giants (All Big)**
9. **Relatives by X**
10. **Quad in Four**
11. **Double Twin Sisters**
12. **Double Twin Brothers**
13. **Double Young & Old**
14. **Double Juniors & Seniors**

Four *Fans*

1. **(Pure) Triple Sisters**

Five *Fans*

1. **Bouquet**
2. **Gem**
3. **Threesomes (All *Pengs*)**
4. ***Peng* Minor Virtues**
5. **Harmonious Mix**
6. **Rainbow**
7. **Family of Five**
8. **Three Numbers**
9. **Blossom Pickers**

Seven *Fans*
1. **Splendid Seven**
2. **Hidden Treasure**

Eight *Fans*
1. ***Peng* Major Virtues**
2. **Two Numbers**

Ten *Fans*
1. **Garden of Flowers**
2. **Pure Breed**
   a. **Royal Jade (All Bamboos)**
   b. **Perfect Coins (All Coins)**
   c. **Imperial Red (All *Wans*)**
3. **Virtuous Winds**
4. **Virgin**
5. **Ace**
6. **Hole in One**

Fifteen *Fans*
1. **Breeze**
2. **Twin Twins (Pure Quadruple Twin Sisters)**

Twenty *Fans*
1. **Hurricane**
2. **Supreme Splendid Seven**

Thirty *Fans*
1. **Thirteen Masters**

Forty *Fans*
1. **Earthly Charms**

Fifty *Fans*
1.   Heavenly Grace

THE PROCEDURES OF HOW TO PLAY THE GAME

The following steps are the order to be accomplished at the start of a game:

SELECTION OF THE SEATING ARRANGEMENT
    Each player occupies a temporary position around the square table.

    Four wind (East, South, West & North) tiles are randomly mixed faced down and stacked them up vertically.

    A volunteer is chosen to roll the pair of dice

    Continuous counting in counterclockwise fashion:
        the dice roller's numbers will then be (1), 5 and 9, for East
        next player to her right, 2, 6, and 10, for South
        opposite her, 3, 7 and 11, for West and
        lastly, to her left, 4, 8 and 12 for North.

The player, whose number matches the score, will be the first to pick the top tile of the earlier randomly stacked tiles of the four winds. Based on the counterclockwise rotation of direction, the next player to pick a tile will be to this player's right. This process of tile picking follows in the same manner until all players have their picks. The player, who picks the East wind from the stacked tiles, will have the sole privilege to pick the seat of his/her choice. This seating arrangement becomes permanent Each of the other players will then go to his/her respective seat according to the wind tile he/she picks: West opposite East, South to East player's right, and North to his/her left. Thus,

SEATING POSITION WITH ITS CORRESPONDING NUMBERS

West (3, 7 & 11)

North (4, 8 & 12)   South (2, 6 & 10)

East (5 & 9)

BUILDING THE WALLS

All players jointly mix the tiles with the picture-sides down.

Each player builds his/her own section of two-stacked high and 18 tile long wall, and places them in front of his/her to form together four-sided wTHE SELECTION OF PERMANENT LEADERSHIP SEAT OR HOME BASE

The player, who picked the east wind tile in the selection process of the seating arrangement, rolls the dice.

The player whose number corresponds to the score becomes the first Wind Position Leader East and his/her seat the Home Base.

THE BREAK SITE

The chosen first Wind Position Leader East, who now represents the permanent leadership seat or Home Base, casts the dice to start the game.

The break-site will be in the wall belonging to the player whose position number in reference to East matches the score of the dice. For example, a score of 5, the break site will be between the fifth and sixth double-stacked tiles, which in this case corresponds to the dice roller's own wall.

This second procedure is unnecessary if on the selection process of the seating arrangement, the score is used to determine the *first* Position Leader East (Home Base) as well as at the same time the break-site (To kill two birds with one stone).

THE DIRECTION OF DRAWS FROM ACTIVE AND INACTIVE WALLS

Active wall (to the left of break-site)   - clockwise

Inactive wall (to the right of break-site)   - counterclockwise

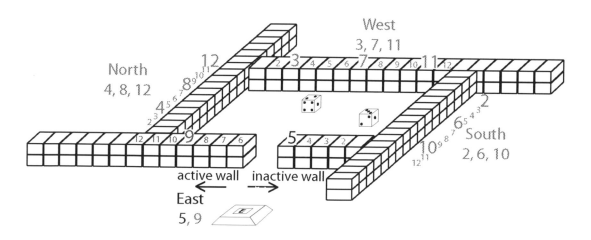

44

THE DEAL

To begin the game, the Position Leader East draws the first two double-stacked (4) tiles from the active wall.

South, West and then North follow likewise in counterclockwise rotation.

Each player draws three times in sequential rotation two double-stacked tiles for a total of twelve.

The Leader East will next draw one tile.

The other three players draw likewise in the same rotational order.

Finally, the leader East draws one more tile before discarding an unwanted tile to start the play and reduce the total number of tiles in his/her concealed Hand to thirteen.

To eliminate this last drawing process, the leader East can simply draw the first and fifth tile at the same time after his/her third draw before the other three players draw their one respective last tile. See diagram below:

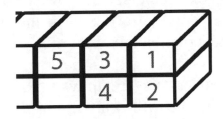

THE PLAY

The play starts on Position Leader East's first discard.

Next, the South player draws a tile from the active wall and discards an unwanted tile from his/her dealt tiles, to be followed in turn by subsequent players according to the counterclockwise rotation: E to S to W to N and back to E in the same directional rotation.

The normal turn of drawing and discarding are temporarily interrupted when a player makes a claim to form a set of *peng/gang* or sequence on the discarded tile.

However, to form a set of sequence, claim on the discarded tile can solely be made by the player whose turn to draw is next, that is, the player to "discarder's" right.

When a discarded tile is claimed by more than one player, the following Priority of Claim Rule applies:

PRIORITY OF CLAIM RULE
A. The player who *mahjongs*. When there is more than one claimant, this right is given to the player whose turn to draw is next in line.
B. The player who *pengs/gangs*.
C. The player who makes sequence. This right can only be exercised by the player who is next in line to draw a tile.

The turn to draw a tile is now resumed by the player to the claimant's right.

The drawing of a decorative (flower/season) tile is instantly exposed and a replacement tile be drawn from the inactive wall before discarding.

In the case of replacements for flower/season tiles at the start of a play, the Claim Order of drawing a tile from the inactive wall follows each player's turn in the same counterclockwise rotation of play.

However, when a player draws another flower/season tile among the replacements, he/she will wait for his/her turn until all other players have gotten theirs in the first turn of draw.

Whenever a player acquires two complete sets of Flower/Season tiles, he/she declares *mahjong* immediately irrespective of the readiness of his/her Hand, and collects double the adopted IFV from the other three players.

Same rule applies for exposing a set of *gang*. However, the timing of its exposure is at the possessor's discretion.

The play of a Hand ends with a player's claim to *mahjong*. The score is settled and a new play starts. The East's leadership position is passed on to the player to his/her right (former South) unless the Leader East him/herself *mahjongs*. In this case, the leadership position remains unchanged.

The Wind of the round changes to the next Wind when the dice is returned to the *first* position leader East, that is, the Home Base.

DIRECTION OF CHANGE OF WIND POSITION LEADER EAST
Counterclockwise: east to   south to   west to   north.

A game is completed when four rounds of wind change have been made and every player has functioned as Position Leader East.

Settlement of Score

In contrast to the Conversion Payment Schedule mentioned in my previously published books (**Mah Jong Unlimited, Mah Jong For Everyone**, and **Mah Jong Fun**), I have now simplified the settlement by making the reward in chips equal to the total *fan* count found in the winning Hand. Thus, 1 *fan* = 1 chip, 12 *fans* = 12 chips, 20 *fans* = 20 chips and so on. Except for the player, who discards the loosing tile, pays double the base amount to the winner. This is also the method used to compute the score in officially sanctioned worldwide Mah Jong competition. In case of the perpetrator of *pao*, the player will be held solely responsible for all payments..

AN OVERVIEW of TJ's VERSION of the MAH JONG GAME

The game is best played with four players.

The goal of play is to achieve one of the following three fundamentals (basic patterns) to *mahjong*:

1. four sets of either sequence*s* and/or *pengs* or *gangs* + a pair;
2. seven pairs;
3. all 13 terminals (end) plus one of these tiles to form the pair.

Prior to the start of the game, following agreements are to be understood by all:

1. list of agreed entities to be used;
2. minimum requirement of *fans* to *mahjong,* for example, no restriction or minimum of 1, 2 or 3 *fan* (*s*);
3. selected method of computation;
4. monetary value of an unit chip;
5. Whether to play for a maximum total *fan* count for a play or n maximum total chip loss for a game.

A Hand's value is based on the total *fan* count of all IFV of each adopted entity upon *mahjong* unless a maximum total *fan* count has been instituted prior to game.

The score in chips is equal to the total *fan* count of a play.

Each player's goal is to construct as many entities as possible for his/her Hand and to be first to *mahjong*.

No limit is set on the number of possible entities, unless everyone concerned specifies a maximum total fan count before the game (that is, the total payment of chips for a winning Hand).

Flower/season tiles are considered "decorative." They are exposed when acquired. They are not used to form sets in Hand, but rightful Flower/Season tiles are each given an IFV which is to be included in the total *fan* count.

An option can be negotiated to have an instant bonus chip to the player upon his/her acquisition of a common decorative tile or set of *peng* of common wind tiles without its inclusion in *fan* counting.

Naming and separating each player's discard is not required. It is each player's own responsibility to pay attention to the discarded tile, which may be placed anywhere on the playing field.

No provision is made to correct the wrong number of tiles in the Hand, once the play has started, but the affected player must remain in the play and obey all game rules. Though this player can no longer *mahjong*, he/she must still obey all rules and responsibilities and pay his/her share to the winner.

Score is settled solely between the winner and the other three players. No score settlement among the losers for entities found in their respective Hands.

After the settlement, a new play is readied with the same process of building walls, dice casting by the Position Leader East, tiles picking and so forth.

No term limit is set for the Position Leader East as long as the player continues to *mahjong*.

Examples of *mahjonged* Hand and computation of its final value

I offer a simulated course of a complete game for my written instruction here.

To facilitate my description of the course progression of the game, I will name the four players East as Edward, South as Samuel, West as Wendy and North as Nancy. Thus, the permanent seating position of each player based on the selection process before a game appears as follows:

Wendy (West)

Nancy (North)   Sam (South)

Ed (East)

Home Base

In contrast, the wind position indicated in () may change after every play, and denotes the position each player holds in reference to wind position leader East at time when a player *mahjongs* . To abbreviate: E = East, S = South, W = West, and N = North

Remark: The sole possession of the dice symbolizes the Position Leader East. This means the passing of the dice to include the wind indicator on changing leadership position to the next player is unnecessary.

It follows that the wind indicator device may remain with the *first* elected Position Leader East (Home Base) for safekeeping throughout the game. This player has the added responsibility to announce the wind change of the round upon the repossession of the dice

Let me begin.

Ed starts the first play of the game by casting the dice. A play is alleged to have proceeded with drawing, discarding, claiming and finally a player's claim to *mahjong*.

Without going into details of the course progress from the Leader East's first discard, each of the following illustrative examples is assumed to be the end stage of a play. A player's winning tile is indicated by **bold X** and the alternate-calling tile is denoted with a plain x.

E1.   Wind round (Round of wind): east.   Sam (S) *mahjongs* on a discarded *wan*

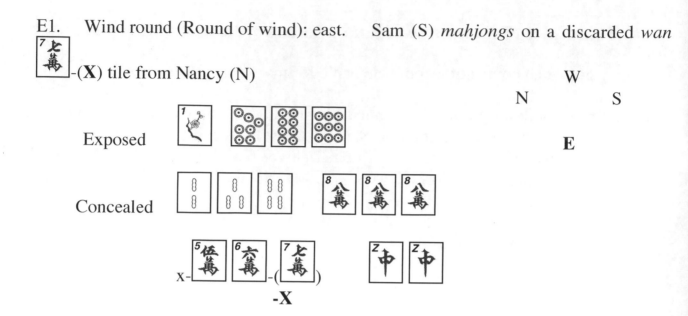

-(**X**) tile from Nancy (N)

Exposed

Concealed

Computation:
Basic *mahjong* (featureless)   2 F
Thus Total *Fan* Count   **2 F**

Remark: I wish to point out that Sam may also *mahjong* on *wan* **4** (-x) without affecting its featureless configuration. Such a featureless Hand is common if no minimum *fan* count to *mahjong* is required as often the case among novice players. In such a case, an agreeable IFV should be negotiated prior to start of game.

Note: Here I suggest to include **Basic Mahjong** as an adopted entity on the agreed List with an assigned *intrinsic fan value* of two *fans*. In other version, no featureless Hand is allowed, and a minimum *fan* count is required in order to go out.

Settlement:
    Nancy (N) pays winner Sam (S) four chips. Ed (E) and Wendy (W) each pays two chips to Sam.

    Position Leader E (possession of dice) is surrendered to east player's right, who was South in the last play, according to the counter clockwise rotation.

E2.   Wind round:east.   Sam (E) discards the losing virtue ⊞(**X**) tile which Ed (now N=former E) claims to *mahjong*.

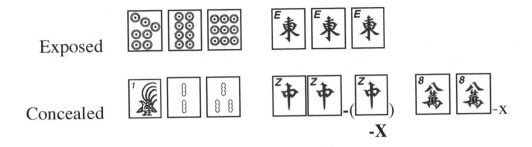

Exposed

Concealed

Computation:

Rainbow	5 F
Peng **a Virtue**	1 F
Peng **Prevalent Wind** (east)	1 F
Eye Pair (8)	1 F
Thus Total *Fan* Count	**8 F**

Remark: Had *wan* 8 timely been replaced with a pair of *wan* 1 or 9, **Mixed End** entity with an IFV of 2 *fans* would have resulted and an additional gain of 1 F in the final count.

Settlement:

Sam (current Position Leader E) pays winner Ed (N) 16 chips and the other two players 8 chips each. The dice are now transferred to Wendy, the player to Position Leader East's right, and who was formerly the South player.

E3.   Wind round east.   Ed (W) **Self-picks** the winning *wan* 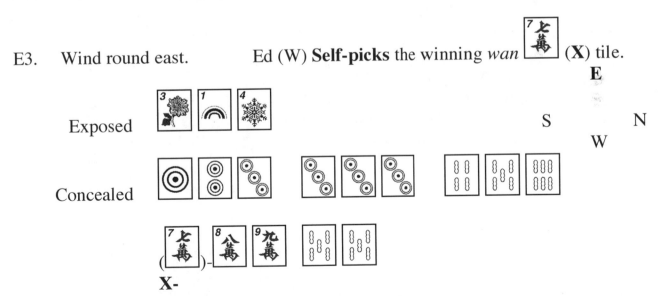 (X) tile.

Computation:

Lucky Strike (**Self-pick** & **Clean Front Door**)	3 F
Mixed Dragon (1-2-3 c 4-5-6 b 7-8-9 w)	2 F
Single (*wan* 7)	1 F

Quad in Two (coin 3)   1 F
Eye Pair (bamboo 5)   1 F
Position (Own) Flower (Chrysumthemun)   1 F
Thus Total *Fan* Count   **9 F**

Settlement:

   Winner Ed (W=former north player of last play) receives 18 chips from every player. Leadership changes to Nancy, former South of last play.

E4.   Wind round east.   Nancy (the current Position Leader E), *mahjongs* on Ed's (now S) discard of *wan* 九萬 (**X**) tile.

                                                          N
                                                      E   W
Exposed   None   S

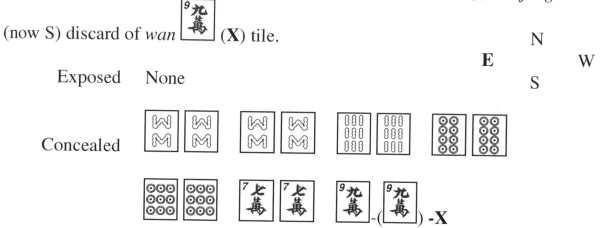

Concealed

Computation:

     Splendid Seven   7 F
     Three Numbers (7, 8, 9)   5 F
     Giants (no tile number below 6)   3 F
     Eye Pairs x 3 (bamboo 8 x 2 & coin 8)   3 F
     Twin Pairs (bamboo 8)   1 F
     Thus Total *Fan* Count   **19 F**

Settlement:

   Ed (S) pays Nancy (E) 38 chips, Sam (W) and Wendy (N) each pays Nancy (E) 19 chips. Nancy (E) retains Position Leadership. **Single** entity can not be claimed nor **Clean Front Door** because the calling or winning tile is always the second mate of the pair and no exposed sets are formed. However, **Lucky Strike** is a valid entity if the winning tile is acquired by **Self-pick**.

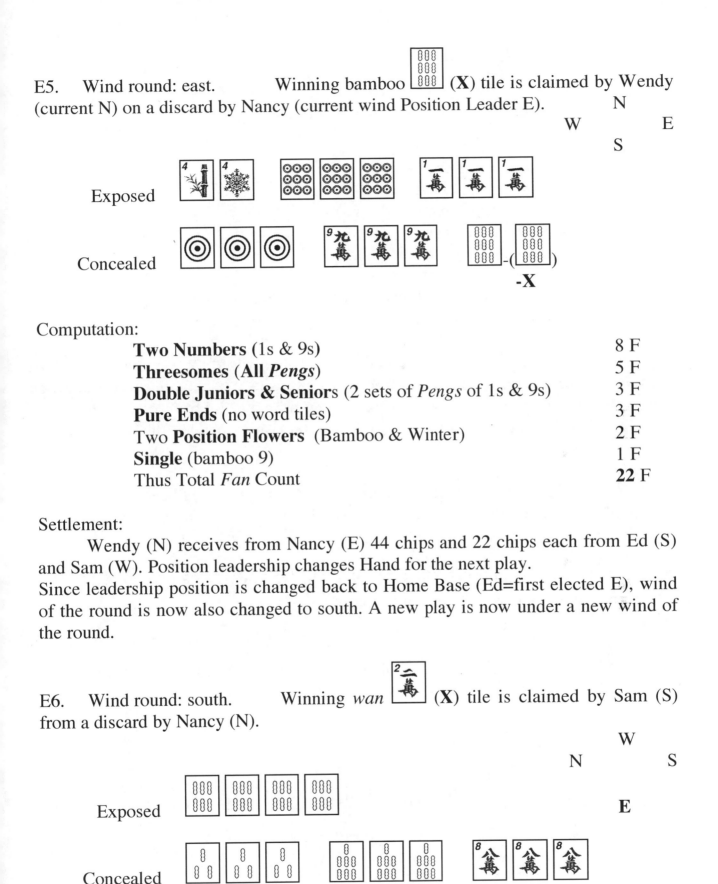

E5.   Wind round: east.   Winning bamboo (**X**) tile is claimed by Wendy (current N) on a discard by Nancy (current wind Position Leader E).

N
W   E
S

Exposed

Concealed

-**X**

Computation:

Two Numbers (1s & 9s)	8 F
Threesomes (**All** *Pengs*)	5 F
Double Juniors & Seniors (2 sets of *Pengs* of 1s & 9s)	3 F
Pure Ends (no word tiles)	3 F
Two **Position Flowers** (Bamboo & Winter)	2 F
Single (bamboo 9)	1 F
Thus Total *Fan* Count	**22** F

Settlement:

Wendy (N) receives from Nancy (E) 44 chips and 22 chips each from Ed (S) and Sam (W). Position leadership changes Hand for the next play.

Since leadership position is changed back to Home Base (Ed=first elected E), wind of the round is now also changed to south. A new play is now under a new wind of the round.

E6.   Wind round: south.   Winning *wan* (**X**) tile is claimed by Sam (S) from a discard by Nancy (N).

W
N   S

E

Exposed

Concealed

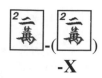

-**X**

Computation:

Hidden Treasure (All self-picked *Pengs*)	7 F
Monocle (second mate of 2)	2 F
Ying Yang (2 numbered suits)	1 F
Chopped (no ends)	1 F
Exposed *Gang*	1 F
Clean (Front Door)	1 F
Poverty (no flower/season, virtue & wind tiles)	1 F
Thus Total *Fan* Count is	**14 F**

Remark: An exposed *Gang* is not considered an exposed set, since it cannot exist in such form in Hand except split up into different sets. (It is similar to the decision when the player foregoes exposing a set of gang from a claim of discard with a set of *peng* in Hand. However, this player will also unwisely abandon the opportunity to draw a replacement tile.)

Note: The entity **Hidden Treasure** is changed to that of **Threesomes** if a set of the 3rd member of *Peng* is obtained from a discard.

Settlement:
       The winner Sam (S) receives 28 chips from Nancy (N) who discards the losing tile, the other two players pay 14 chips each.

E7.   Wind round: south.   Winning east wind [西] (**X**) tile is **Self-pick** by Nancy (W).

Exposed   None

Concealed

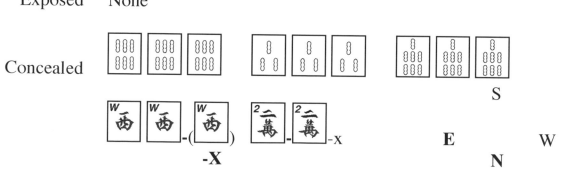

-**X**

E   W

S

N

Computation:
Hidden Treasure		7 F
Lucky Strike		3 F
Peng **Position Wind** (west)		1 F
Eye Pair (2)		1 F
Thus Total *Fan* Count		**12 F**

Note: **Hidden Treasure** entity is applicable only if the origin of all sets of **Threesomes** in Hand are acquired by player him/herself including the winning tile, except when calling **Single** for the pre-requisite pair as in E3. Otherwise, the applicable entity is that of **Threesomes** but claim of **Eye Pair** entity remains valid.

Settlement:
    All players pay the winner Nancy (W) twice the base amount of 12 chips. Leadership position moved to the next player.

E8.   **Wind round south.**   Nancy (S) claims the winning coin 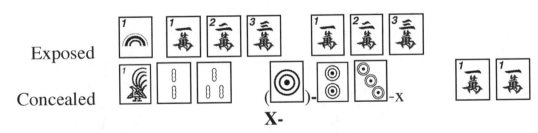 (X) tile on Sam's (N) "act" to add this tile to his earlier exposed set of *peng*.

E
S   N
W

Computation
Three Numbers (1s 2s & 3s)		5 F
Dwarfs (all numbers in sets below 4)		3 F
Relatives by 1 (all sets have 1 tile)		3 F
Pure Ends (no word tiles)		3.F
Mixed Triple Sisters (1-2-3 b c w)		2 F
Quad in Three (*wan* 1's in 3 sets)		2 F
Twin Sisters (1-2-3 w)		1 F
All Sequences (all sets in numerical order)		1 F
Piracy (coin 1claimed from exposing set of *gang*)		1 F
Orphan (*mahjonged* on last available tile)		1 F

57

Thus Total *Fan* Count **22 F**

Settlement:

Nancy (S) receives 44 chips from Sam (N) and 22 chips each from Wendy (E) and Ed (W). This winner also assumes the leadership position to start the next play.

Comment: Ambitious player would not *mahjong* on coin 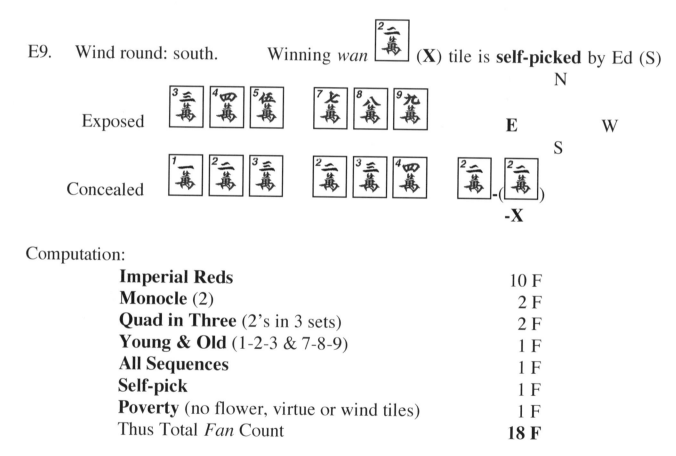 (**X**) tile, since the total *fan* count of this Hand will be greatly reduced by the loss of the IFV of half of the above-mentioned entities, to wit, **Three Numbers**, **Relatives by 1**, **Mixed Triple Sisters**, **Piracy** and **Orphan**, for a total not less than 12 *fans*.

E9.   Wind round: south.   Winning *wan* (**X**) tile is **self-picked** by Ed (S)

Computation:

Imperial Reds	10 F
Monocle (2)	2 F
Quad in Three (2's in 3 sets)	2 F
Young & Old (1-2-3 & 7-8-9)	1 F
All Sequences	1 F
Self-pick	1 F
Poverty (no flower, virtue or wind tiles)	1 F
Thus Total *Fan* Count	**18 F**

Note: Observant reader will see that instead of claiming the **Monocle** entity, the winning Hand can equally be viewed as having **Single** and **Eye Pair** entities with equal total *fans* as the hidden group can be arranged as sets of 1-**x**-3, 2-3-4 and **2-2**.

Settlement:

Every player pays Ed (S) 36 chips. The leadership position is transferred to this player to start the new play. The dice have now returned to Home Base (Ed=first elected E). Wind of the round is thus changed to next round of wind: west.

E10. Wind round: West.   Wendy (W) discarded the loosing virtue 發 (**X**) tile, which was claimed by Ed (E).

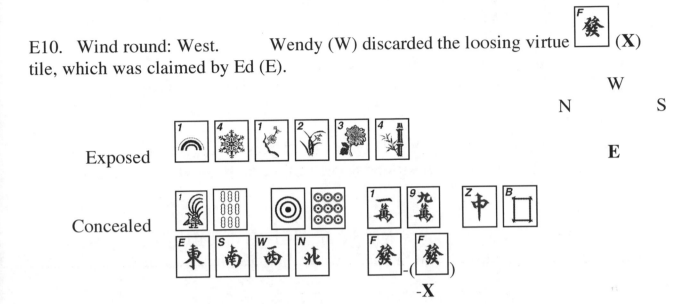

Computation:
Thirteen Masters	30 F
Bouquet	5 F
2 Position (Own) Flowers (Spring & Plum)	2 F
Thus Total *Fan* Count	**37 F**

Settlement:
    Wendy (W) pays Ed (E) 74 chips. Ed (E) receives 37 chips from Sam (S) and Nancy (N) each. Ed (E) retains his wind leadership position.

E11. Wind round: west.   Winning *wan* 八萬 (**X**) tile is claimed by Wendy (W) from a discard by Nancy (N).

59

Computation:

Harmonious Mix	5 F
Mixed Ends	2 F
Young & Old (1-2-3 & 7-8-9 x 2)	2 F
Peng **a Virtue**	1 F
Single (8)	1 F
Twin (7-8-9 & 7-8-9)	1 F
Thus Total *Fan* Count	**12 F**

Settlement:

Nancy (N) pays Wendy (W) 24 chips. Ed (E) and Sam (S) each pay 12 chips to the winner. The leadership position is now again changed to the next player.

E12. Wind round: west. Winning coin (**X**) tile is acquired by Wendy (S) from a replacement tile from the inactive wall after exposing a flower

Exposed

Concealed

Computation:

Family of Fives (5 in all sets)	5 F
Three Numbers (5s, 6s & 7s)	5 F
Blossom Picker (specific coin 5)	5 F
Triple Sisters (5-6-7 b c w)	3 F
Twin (5-6-7 x2 *wan*)	1 F
All Sequences	1 F
Chopped	1 F
Position Flower (Orchid)	1 F
Thus Total *Fan* Count	**22 F**

Settlement:

Wendy (S) collects 44 chips from every player and assumes the leadership position.

Note: If Wendy *mahjongs* from a discard, the right claim of entity will be that of **Monocle** and not **Blessing**.

E13. Wind round: west. Ed (W) claimed the discarded coin (**X**) tile from Wendy (E).

E

S   N

W

Exposed

Concealed

X-

Computation:

***Peng* Minor Virtues** (2 sets of *pengs*)	5 F
Harmonious Mix (suit +word tiles)	5 F
Mixed Ends (all sets of hard tiles)	2 F
Twin (2 sets of 7-8-9)	1 F
Single (*wan* 7)	1 F
Thus Total *Fan* Count	**14 F**

Settlement:

Ed (W) received from Wendy (E) 28 chips, and 14 chips each from Sam (N) and Nancy (S). Leadership is changed to the next player.

E14. Wind round: west. Ed (S) discarded the losing coin (**x**) tile on which Nancy (E) *Mahjongs*.

N

E   W

S

Exposed

Concealed

Computation:

Rainbow (all 5 suits)		5 F
Threesomes (**All** *Pengs*)		5 F
Mixed Ends (sets of hard tiles)		2 F
Peng **a Virtue** (set of *fa* tiles)		1 F
Single (coin 9)		1F
Peng **Prevalent Wind** (west)		1 F
Position Flower (Spring)		1 F
Thus Total *Fan* Count		**16 F**

Settlement:

Ed (S) pays Nancy (E) 32 chips. Wendy (N) and Sam (W) each pay the winner 16 chips. Leadership position remains unchanged.

E15. Wind round: west. Winner Sam (W) *mahjongs* on a discard of bamboo

 (x) tile from Nancy (E).

```
        N
    E       W
        S
```

Exposed: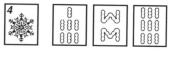

Concealed: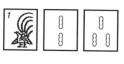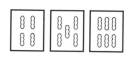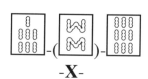

-X-

Computation:

Royal Jade (Pure Breed)		10 F
Pure Dragon (1-2-3, 3-4-5, 7-8-9)		3 F
Quad in Three (8)		2 F
Twin (7-8-9)		1 F
All Sequences		1 F
Eye Pair (8)		1 F
Single (8)		1 F
Thus Total *Fan* Count		**19 F**

Settlement:

Sam (W) collects 38 chips from Nancy (E) and 19 chips each from Ed (S) and Wendy (N). Wind position leadership is again transferred back to Home base (Ed), the wind of the round is thus also changed to next wind, which will be north.

E16. Wind round: north.   Nancy (N) claims the discarded virtue 發 (**X**) tile by Wendy (W) to *mahjong*.

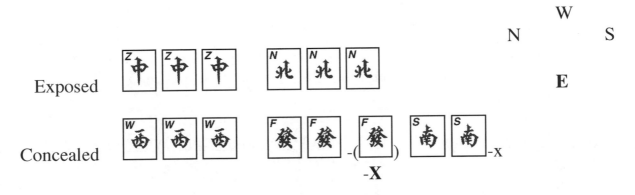

Computation:

Virtuous Winds (word tiles)	15 F
Peng **2 Virtues** (2 sets of v tiles)	2 F
Peng **Prevalent Wind** (north)	1 F
Peng **Position Wind** (north)	1 F
Thus Total *Fan* Count	19 F

Settlement:

Wendy (W) pays Nancy (N) 38 chips. Ed (E) and Sam (S) each pay Nancy (N) 19 chips. Position leadership is transferred to the next player, who was Sam (S)

E17. Wind round: north.   Nancy (W) claims his/her winning *wan* 三萬 (x) tile from Ed's (N) discard.

Computation:

Harmonious Mix (suit + word tiles)	5 F
Peng **Prevalent Wind** (north)	1 F
Peng **Position Wind** (west)	1 F
Young & Old (1-2-3 & 7-8-9 *wan*)	1 F
Single (3)	1 F
Eye Pair (5)	1 F
Thus Total *Fan* Count	**11 F**

Settlement:

Nancy (W) collects 22 chips from Ed (N) and 11 chips each from Sam (E) and Wendy (S). This former South player is now to start the next play as the new position leader.

E18. Wind round north.   Ed (W) *mahjongs* on Wendy's (E) discard of bamboo (x) tile.

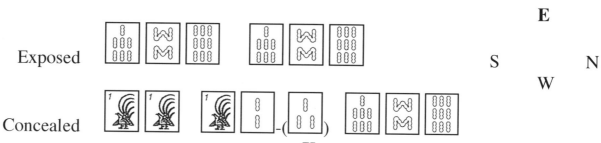

Computation:

Royal Jade (Pure Breed)	10 F
Pure (Identical) Triple Sisters (7-8-9 x3)	4 F
Pure Ends (hard tiles of 1 suit)	3 F
Young & Old (1-2-3 & 7-8-9) x 3	3 F
All Sequences	1 F
Single (bamboo 3)	1 F
Thus Total *Fan* Count	**22 F**

Settlement:

Wendy (E) pays Ed (W) 44 chips; Nancy (S) and Sam (N) each pay Ed (W) 22 chips. Position leadership moves to the next player, who is Nancy

Quiz: What would the total *fan* count be, had Ed *mahjonged* on bamboo [image] tile? Concealed Hand can also be arranged to call as having 1-1-1 and 2-x. See footnote below.[9]

E19. Wind round north. Nancy (E) *mahjongs* on **Self-pick** of coin [一萬] (X)
tile from the last tile of wall.

                          N
                   E   W
                         S

Exposed   [9萬][9萬][9萬] [Z中][Z中][Z中] [F發][F發][F發]

                  [B][B][B]

Concealed   [1萬]-([1萬])
                  -**X**

Computation:

Major Virtues (3 sets of *peng* virtues)	8 F
Threesomes (all *pengs*)	5 F
Harmonious Mix (1 suit + word)	5 F
Mixed Ends (sets of hard tiles)	2 F
Miracle (*mahjong* on last tile)	2 F
Thus Total *Fan* Count	**22** F

Settlement:
    Nancy (E) receives from everybody 44 chips. Position leadership stays put.

E20. Wind round: north. Nancy (E) **Self-picks** the winning coin [2二萬] (x) tile.

Exposed:

---

9   Gain of **Monocle** entity, does not compensate for loss of IFV for **Pure Ends**, **Young & Old**, **All Sequences** and **Single**, a net loss of 6 *fans*.

Concealed: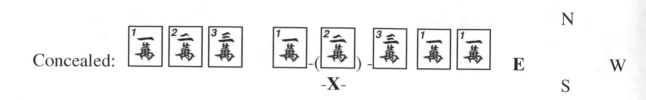

Computation:

Three Numbers (1s, 2s, 3s)	5 F
Dwarfs (**All Small**)	3 F
Triple Sisters (1-2-3 b c w)	3 F
Pure Ends (all sets with hard tiles)	3 F
Quad in Three (4 1's in 3 sets)	2 F
Relatives by 1	3 F
Twin (2 sets of 1-2-3 *wan* tiles)	1 F
Single (*wan* 2)	1 F
All Sequences	1 F
Self-pick (*wan* 2)	1 F
Poverty (no decorative or word tiles)	1 F
Thus Total *Fan* Count	**24 F**

Settlement:

Each player pays Nancy (E) 48 chips.

Leadership position thus again remains unchanged. And one more new play is to be started for the last wind round.

Comment: Observant reader would note that had the winner *mahjonged* on *wan*

tile, claim of entities for **Relatives by 1**, **Pure Ends**, **Twin** and **All Sequences** would have been lost. (The concealed sets in Hand would be viewed as having 123, 111, 3-3 (x).

To alleviate my reader's anguish for needing to add all these IFV of numerous entities, I suggest as in my practice to simply separate equal number of tiles for each entity when computing. For example, put aside 5 tiles for entity **Three numbers**, 3 tiles for **Dwarfs**, 3 tiles for **Triple Sisters** and so on, and then add all the tiles in the group for the total *fan* count.

E21. Wind round: north.   Sam (W) *mahjongs* on Wendy's (N) discard of
(**X**) tile.

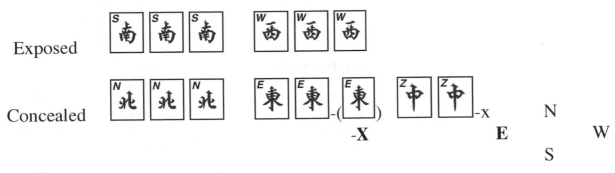

Exposed

Concealed

                          -X   E   N   W
                                                  S

Computation:

Heavenly Grace	50 F
Thus Total *Fan* Count	**50 F**

Settlement:

Sam (W) receives 100 chips from Wendy (N) and 50 chips each from Ed (S) and Nancy (E). Sam's achievement for this Hand is similar to winning the $1,000,000.00 jackpot in a Las Vegas casino.

In summary, there are 21 plays in 4 round of wind changes. Of these illustrative Hands, Edward won 6 plays, Samuel completed 4 Hands, Wendy went out on 3 occasions and Nancy *mahjonged* 8 times. At the end of the game, Edward claimed to have won 80 chips. Samuel is short of 103 chips. Wendy is in the red for 292 chips. Nancy has a net surplus of 315 chips more than her base capital. Thus the two winners, Edward and Nancy, together won for a total of 395 chips, which is the exact combined amount the two losers, Samuel and Wendy paid out.

I have described the completion of four rounds of wind changes and that every player has served as position leader East, I find it most proper to conclude my written instruction here.

May my readers have now learned and understood how features can be created ad infinitum based on unchanging fundamentals and experience the exciting joy upon the accomplishment of an exceptionally exotic feature such as **Thirteen Masters, Supreme Splendid Seven** or other uncommon, beautiful entities! It is no exaggeration to compare with the lasting joyful experience of a golfer who hits hole in one.

Computation practice from real *mahjonged* Hands

The following examples are from real Hands and assumed to have gone out on tile **x** from non-exposed tiles in Hand, those exposed set of tiles are formed in the course of play.

E1. Exposed: bamboo 1-2-3, coin 1-1-1 tiles
Concealed: *wan* 1-2-3, & 1-1, coin 1-**x**-3. Winner went out on a discarded coin 2.

Computation:		
Dwarfs		5 F
Triple Sisters (123 b, 123 c & 123 *w*)		3 F
Relatives of 1		3 F
Pure Ends		1 F
Mixed Twin (123 b & 123 *w*)		1 F
Quad in Two (coin 1s)		1 F
Single (coin 2)		1 F
All Sequences		1 F
Poverty		1 F
Thus, the total is		**17 F**

E2. Exposed: coin 3-4-5 and 4-5-6, *wan* 5-6-7tiles
Concealed: *wan* 5-6-7 and 5-**x** **Player** *mahjongs* on a discarded *wan* 5.

Computation:		
Family of 5		5 F
Twin Sisters (5-6-7 *wan*)		1 F
Monocle (*wan* 5)		2 F
Yin Yang		1 F
Thus, the total is		**11F**

E3. Exposed: bamboo 4-5-6
Concealed: 4-5-6, 4-5-6. x-4-5-x & 5-5. This Hand goes out on **Self-pick** bamboo 3.

Computation:		
One Suit		10 F
Family of Fives		5 F
Pure Triple Sisters		4 F
Twin		1 F
Chopped		1 F
All Sequences		1 F

Self-pick	1 F
Eye Pair	1 F
Thus, the total *fan* count is	**24 F**

Comment: Had the winning player did not self-pick the calling tile, it is worth the risk to wait for bamboo 6 to complete the Hand. Since the total *fan* count will increase with the inclusion no less of the I*F*V of entities of **Three Numbers** and **Twin Twins!**

E4.   Exposed: coins 6-7-8
Concealed: 6-7-8, 6-7-8, 6-7-8 coins & 8-*x wans*, This Hand goes out on single 8 of **Eye Pair**.

Computation:		
	Twin Twins	15 F
	Three Numbers	5 F
	Giants	3 F
	Quad in Four	3 F
	Relatives by 8	3 F
	Monocle (8)	2 F
	Yin Yang	1 F
	Sequences	1 F
	Chopped	1 F
Thus, the total *fan* count is		**34 F**

.E5.   Exposed: *wan* 1-2-3, 1-2-3
Concealed:1-2-3 bamboos, 1-2-3, coins, 1-1 & 1-2-x *wans*. This Hand goes out on single *wan* 3.

Computation:		
	Three Numbers	5 F
	Triple Sister (coins)	4 F
	Mixed Triple Sisters (c b w)	3 F
	Relatves by 1	3 F
	Dwarfs	3 F
	All Ends	2 F
	Single	1 F
	Sequences	1 F
Thus, the total *fan* count is		**23 F**